GROUND WATER

Matthew Hollis

GROUND WATER

BLOODAXE BOOKS

ISBN: 978 1 85224 657 0

First published 2004 by
Bloodaxe Books Ltd,
Highgreen,
Tarset,
Northumberland NE48 1RP.

Fifth impression 2008

www.bloodaxebooks.com
For further information about Bloodaxe titles
please visit our website or write to
the above address for a catalogue.

Bloodaxe Books Ltd acknowledges
the financial assistance of
Arts Council England, North East.

Printed in Great Britain by
Bell & Bain Limited, Glasgow, Scotland.

for Dad

i.m.

Acknowledgements

My thanks are due to the editors of the following publications in which some of these poems first appeared: *Chatter of Choughs* (Signal Books, 2001), *ibid, Island City* (Broad Street Poetry, 1999), *Love for Love* (Morning Star/Polygon, 2000), *The North, Oxford Magazine, Oxford Poetry, Parenthesis, PN Review, Poetry London, Poetry Review, Reactions 1 & 2* (Pen&inc, 2000 & 2001). In addition, some of these poems were first broadcast on BBC Radio. 'The Fielder' appeared in a private press edition from Clutag Press, 2002. 'One Man Went to Mow' was a prize winner in the National Poetry Competition, 1996. *The Boy on the Edge of Happiness* (Smith/Doorstop Books, 1996) was a prize winner in the Poetry Business Competition, 1995. 'Wake' borrows from 'Song (Sweetest love, I do not goe)' by John Donne.

Additional thanks are due to the Society of Authors for an Eric Gregory Award in 1999 and, along with the Arts Council and the Camden Trust, for their support in the *First Lines* poetry tour, 2001. My thanks to Ron Costley.

For their criticism and advice on this manuscript I am grateful to Simon Armitage, John Burnside, Polly Clark, Antony Dunn and Paul Keegan; and to Rebecca O'Connor, who gave it all a name.

Contents

GROUND WATER

Wintering

If I close my eyes I can picture him
flitting the hedgerow for splints
or a rib of wood to kindle the fire,

or reading the snow for whatever
it was that came out of the trees
and circled the house in the night;

if I listen I can hear him out
in the kitchen, scudding potatoes,
calling the cat in; if I breathe

I can smell the ghost of a fire,
a burning of leaves that would fizz
in the mizzle before snow.

There is in this house now
a stillness of cat fur and boxes,
of photographs, paperbacks, waste-

paper baskets; a lifetime
of things that I've come here
to winter or to burn.

There is in this world one snow fall.
Everything else is just weather.

The Orchard Underwater

Dragging for a place to catch the line,
I'm drawn back for a moment to the nearwater
by a clatter of choughs climbing off the headland
aiming somewhere for God.
                       This is no trick of aeronautics
but the genuine effect – God's Flyers, you called them,
           inking the air with trial after trial,
localised as downpour, a pencil of rain.
                        And yet,
what we remembered of these waters:
the cove in which the minke beached,
the pitchpoles of the bottle-nose,
one capsize, a storm or so; and
once, a raft of apples came
                bobbing round the bay –
we didn't know it then but they were
tipped into the sea by men
                   with memories of home,
a place that slipped away one year
           they dammed and sealed the valley floor,
an orchard sending up its fruit
                  like life-floats or some SOS;
           which might have been the last of it,
but some time on, in bony drought,
                     the lane rose from the lake,
and folk came from their homes again
                   to walk among themselves;
past cattle pens, apple pots, the schoolroom
      trapped with fish;
               like time given back, offered over again;
as if all the words they failed to say
were spilled out on the quay and claimed

like undelivered letters finding home;
                                    as if
we'd tapped our own lost tongue,
and stirred it into flight;
                    as if the sea
were rolled up like a carpet on the hillside,
and the sun had scissored out the sky
                                    and left it to one side,
and we had all the world to patch together
                                    in whatever order,
some fuzzy-felt, or stickle-brick
                            to set out as we'd choose it;
as if my steps could be with yours, as if we could
forgive ourselves, and take some second chance
before the rains
                    re-close on the chapel yard
and all I can taste is a crab hand of apples;
all that I see, that unkind flight to God;
all that I hear, the eerie tide
            of a church bell moving in the swell,
                        calling the waters to prayer.

Clearance

(for Sophie Goldsworthy)

We came with cases packed full of ourselves –
our cuckoo tongues, our Sunday clothes –
on drovers' tracks to the cattle docks
and the ships pointing into tomorrow.
We kept our language low, and tasted
the new words; our working knowledge
of land folk, the old songs, the kinder
jokes, already a shorthand, a history.

Almost the last of the last behind:
a garron, two shelties, a froth of chickens,
until all that remains is a family of slaters
and a dust-bunny skeltering over the boards
for the jamb of an open door, where it snags
on something almost perceptible.

The Fielder
(for Kim Walwyn)

The day is late, later than the sun.
He tastes the dusk of things and eases down,
and feels the shade set in across the yard.
He never thought there'd be so much undone,
so much in need of planing: the haugh unmown
with its fist of bracken, the splinting of the cattle bar,
the half-attended paddock wall
scribbled with blackthorn and broke-wool.

Perhaps he could have turned the plough for one last till,
be sure, or surer, of where the seeding fell.
But then it's not the ply that counts, but the depth of furrow,
knowing the take was deep and real, knowing the change was made.
And field by field the brown hills harvest yellow.
And few of us will touch the landscape in that way.

The Small Rain Down Can Rain

I

Last night the sea clouds came inland
with darkened sails, sacks of rain.
Morning, we woke in a Cavan town
to a sweat of salt, and the afterthought
of things left out at night: the dulled paint,
salined cars, a white tide on a pair of shoes.

Watching it busying at the window
we knew the rain could not get in,
so light in spray you could seem
to go about your business and stay dry.
And down in your garden we went about ourselves:
picking through the raspberry harm,
the fallen elms, the oiling stream,
your skirt gathered about yourself
to keep the hem from wetting.

But how the small rain down can rain –
so tiny in its feet we barely note
its passage through the fibres and pores
until suddenly it's overcoming, at the skin;
a reminder how little that is outside
stays that way for long.

II

Not the telephone call, or the news itself,
not the unmarked roads of Carnaross,
not the service, or the bluebells, but this:
the legs that bore the coffin. Seven struts
were planted square, but one was squint
to the stone floor, its back leg cocked; as if,
even then, you were straining to contribute,
or lifting the latch to the next room.

The River Drivers

*DRIVE n. & vb. bringing a harvest of lumber or pulpwood
from the forest down a spring-swollen river to the mill.
Men work the* drive; *the logs are* driven; *the man who
works the drive is a* river-driver.

– JOHN GOULD, Maine Lingo

I can hear the haul coming out of the forest
on frozen sleds for the landing grounds,
canting the cold wood into the boom
waiting for the winter's crack.
                Spring,
                        just,
the river still shouldering ice,
and already we're beginning the drive
to bring this lumber in.
                From here to the mill,
we will walk the water
on a cargo of pulpwood and timber
with only a pikepole and the caulks on our boots
                    to balance,
rounding, rolling the forest on –
birlers, shepherds of the river.
                    To know her.
Where her currents beat swiftly,
where she slows
            brought to,
                  where she tapers, lullies.
Where to place the men,
                when to move them on,
to keep the drive from grounding.
Nothing is more dangerous than the grounding.
Where the woods and the river
go against each other

                              to find out which is stronger.
In a thousand logs,
                    just one is king –
that one removed will set the whole jam flowing.
But get it wrong and all go under.
I've watched men slip
                         through a gate in the river,
and I wake at night to what they must have seen:
looking up at a surface
                         grown over with trees.
On one man's body was a letter to his lover
with just enough saved to bring them together.
And the story tells that she stood on a loch side
watching the mailboat inch towards her,
bringing the words that he couldn't deliver.
                                            And, sure,
there's a quieter life than this
                                  at camp,
waking to the gut-hammer:
the smith lays out the day's repairs,
a canthook, some shodding, a whiffletree;
a filer sets the dull saws singing;
a chopper checks his swing for jounce,
weighing the yield of the new carved handle.
And none of them is coming home,
none will ride the river.
                          Some will fever
in the arms of the forest;
                           and only the sound
of the gorby bird might turn them around,
or a coydog's trail to camp.
                             But I can find
no home in this, no matter to believe.
And what we need is a reason for going back,
for taking the odds again and again

               leaping
                          from
                                      log
                   to
            log
chancing the meltwater, chancing it all,
burning our insides on the nightly spirits
drinking to forget the day.
      And tomorrow or the next
                                    when the drive
                                               jams –
and it comes to me to pick which log to free,
to draw lots once more with the river –
at this moment I will think of you
waiting home or at the mill,
                          busying yourself
in the day's small hands,
               making the water ground.
                                    And I know
I cannot get this wrong.
                              But fold these words
in case the mailboat comes
      and there's no cause to land.
         Then let the river drive on,
                          past lamp husk,
sawdust, and out to the ocean,
where the jaw of the sea drops
                              and,
tasting the vastness of the open water,
      the last lobster boats think twice
            and turn in again for home.

Nymph

if
like your body
the sea were a body
then what is this I feel
as yard by yard
you descend into its arms
a slip of water
between your thighs
around your waist
the hands of the ocean
drawing you out
losing your step
in the dance

Winter Break

White at midnight – all is new, as if
the world began today. The fields are thick
and neatly tucked, the birds have packed,
a dog gives up its man and goes;
and all the towns are choked and closed,
pinned in place by wooden poles,
no last train home, no chaser for the road.

No one knows what's lost beneath the snow,
what ways gave up to way, what water flowed,
what change of place there really was,
what change in us, what roughing frost;
and nothing kills nor is killed off, but winters
from the thaw; like snowmen getting up to go,
whose love is cold, whose love not cold enough.

᷎

not even the leaves
can lay down with such gentleness
or be touched so lightly as by your touch

in which I am, very simply, uncurling
as a leaf uncurls in first spring, or
folded, unfolds in your opening palm

which should you not want, I will curl
instead as a leaf curls towards fall
folding over and over itself

and you will go by
and the winter will echo
enormously

Skin Contact

Beyond the gravel and the clay-stone stile,
where the small town narrows to a model,

I step into the vines and the last night air
and wait for the dawn to come about.

In a loosening outhouse, in a flunk of linen,
you are still to the morning, not yet of this day,

and nothing should hurry you around;
not the sound of the milk-van or the baker's kiln,

not the cockerel, and not my own hand;
though the sky is beginning to bruise,

and citrus lights the far field vines,
and, humbly, there's a coming into colour:

the thin church, the reed of trees,
the green air whittling the river-grass,

stirring the first insects to gauze.
                                    Watching this

is to realise how little comes of urgency,
how little worth-its-weight is, in the end, waitless:

the vineyards speckled with half-remembered homes,
their ghost of families, their trellis grounds,

so carefully sown and stitched and torn, so
precisely brought to handle; where the must of pulp

is honeyed into ferment; where the skin is sensitive
and contact is measured to the minute –

that teasing brush with the body, unlocking
the tannins, opening the window of the wine.

Like the ullage – the breathing space I could never judge –
the balance of touch has undone us: that striking of patience

between presence and space, heat and the necessary calm.
No bottle worth its glass came from any less devotion.

And because you would not wait as I would wait
I settle instead for the gentlest reminders:

your flint of eyes, your pallor skin, your nettling
touched, but left untrampled, and barely stung.

In you more than you

the lines of a lifetime gather like water.
In places these streams are a torrent,
a raging flood, a sweeping away;
in places a careful shallow, a rockpool
still as a mirror. What I see in you is me:
an image of myself complete, as one,
more real than I could ever be.
What I see in you I cannot live to,
too much the perfect picture of myself.
So I will leave, and leave to you
the fragments of the me I seem,
this hem of guesses and glue. I'm not
the me I thought I was, and tell you so.
Pass round the pieces and let them go.

Hi-Fidelity

Finally, he showed her how to weight the arm
on a fulcrum so true the needle
had only to ghost on the vinyl,
with each revolution threading into itself
for a sound so honest it defied comprehension;
the 78s of trainsong and birdcall
like a passing tremor, or a flight of sunlight,
spoken recordings so faithful she'd vow
that was company beyond the wall
but for the sound of the needle's own
entrance and exit – for all the world
the open and close of a back door.

The Sour House

Through the frost-hole of the passenger window
your tenant's house is ringed in winter.
He's turning the snow from the path

that lay in the night. He can far less
handle a spade than you, dipping the lug
as though the shovel itself was unbalanced.

And what you found inside you would not forget:
room on room of bottled milk, gagging
the stairwell, the hallway, bookshelves,

like a stumbled-on ice world, a sweep of winter.
For years he maintained the world his parents left,
taking in milk he never drank. Evenings spent out

in the yard, piecing apart the Ford his father drove –
sill-lines, cogwheels, dippers fanned round him,
working each burr to a touch.

For years I coloured your world in hues
you didn't recognise; never your island,
always your skerry – 'unable to see

the romance of the thing for the thing itself'.
That, airing his house, the rancour
would catch as far as the common;

and what you found in the garage was scrap:
not the showpiece I'd imagined but the pin
pulled out, a car returned to the sum of its parts.

Driving now through the cloughs at dusk
I am struck by the things *I* can't let go;
that some things weal on the body like braille –

the sight of you just home from the milk-house
matted and choking, your raw nose streaming,
gutting the fridge in two clean strokes –
like a swimmer striking out for land.

Isostasy

ISOSTASY n. Equilibrium or stability
due to equality of (hydrostatic) pressure

And another thing I didn't say:
that the upward mass of a cresting wave
will always momentarily equate
to the average human being's weight;
so that if your timing is exact,
your footfall strict, and you've cracked
the basic rudiments of fetch,
you can run across the sea from one edge
to another on a causeway made
of temporality and water. Please mind
to keep that close next time the scale
has got too broad to broach, the pale
well passed beyond; and come down then
against your coast to hear the sound of feet
run in across the rooftops of the sea.
This much is truth, in principle at least.

It Rains During the Night

So I am reminded of that tale
    of the hill man who'd never seen sea
        and how one day he opened his door
            to look out on nothing but ocean –

the road to the village and the village gone,
    nothing so much as a path or a lawn
        just the sea lapping the flagstone
            waving him in like so many cupped hands.

There is in this story, of course, a flaw,
    a flaw of not insubstantial demands.
        But sometimes I wake in a nightroom
            after you've gone, to a perfume of salt,

seawater beading the boards; listening to the lap
    of out-things getting in – which surely would stop
        if ever I would venture to open the door
            and step out on the might-be of water.

Sandwriting

And so we let this go –
bottle after bottle, we pour away
all that we came to distil;
a spirit of things, and of you,
that will prick on my tongue
long after you've taken this leave.

Tonight I sat to write the poem
you'd not see, the letter you'd not open,
and raised a glass to you, sweet you,
who'd not raise one to me.
On the last news before closedown
they were lifting a boat from a Cromarty bed,
four men two months on the sea floor.
A thousand ships had pulled their anchor
and sailed that day; and one, just one,
went down all hands, like it fell
through a hole in the ocean.

There is no country, no geography between us,
but that which we ourselves map:
a tangle of rivers and bridle tracks,
a thumbprint of mountains all cardboard and crepe.
The landscape that matters we carry within us,
like a blueprint for water – an endless
flow of all things to each other.
So when, in just hours, you wake to a breathing
that is not your own, and is not mine,
may you think on the space between us
as nothing at all but that which we draw,
like a line in the sand at the edge of the sea.

Somewhere out on this night
you have emptied the air and left it to dry.
No gull-calls, no shiphorns, just the lull
of the sea, and the last of last night's malt.
In those grains of peat sod and kelp
I found you – shimmered and soured,
unmistakably tart; those rites that once
we took only together were my pursuit alone.
And, senseless to your whereabouts, I drank instead
to each single letter of your name; wave
after wave, till the spirit puckered and blunt.

An hourglass tipped on its side is forever.
And for her, who said the sands were against us,
I went down to the shore in the moments before dawn
and wrote the five letters of her name,
and waited the tide that would come and efface them;
as one by one the oil lamps wicked across the bay
like a hundred homes standing up, to be counted.

And let us say
(for Emma McKiernan, on her birth, 8/9/99)

That if the linen flapped too loud
The washing line was taken down

And if a shopdoor bell was rung
Its tongue was held with cotton thumbs

And if a milkfloat tattled by
It was flagged down and held aside

And should the rivers drown us out
We had them dammed at every mouth

And coughed our engines gently off
And wrapped our tyres in woollen socks

And sat awhile on silent roads
Or dawdled home in slippered shoes

And did not sound but held our tongues
And watched our watches stop, and startle on.

Harwonder

Perhaps it was the way we caddied the sound,
or delighted at its invention.

But more likely it was the sharing of a word
that no one else knew –

a language for two, putting a name
to what we have between us –

'harwonder', a term of no strict definition,
but intimately ours –

                    musical, made up of us;
where language was a kind of touch, a pull

as inevitable as any vinyl's concentric,
a groove we could not depart from.

And even before you spoke of being
unable to fight it any more

I had long since given myself up to you
and your perfect pitch.

And you lead me through, and into you,
to feel a slow crescendo;

and all and two-thirds of the world
was tuning-up beneath our feet

converging on a single note.

Blink

as your eye closes (slowly
like canopy lowering to rain,
or wing touching a far floor,
shedding a slightest, most fragile tear,
the shape of wave, the shape of breaker, un-
breaking across a round sea, to somewhere
shore, where I am stood and, seeing, find
in you I hope, my reflection,
unmistakably, in your paper-
weight look, in your closed
eye) and opens

Two Kinds

The fox knows many things,
but the hedgehog knows one big thing.

         – ARCHILOCHUS, Fragments

And yes, I suppose I thought myself the fox
who knew so many small things of its world;
that there's more than one way to cross a field,
more than one break in the fence.

So imagine my surprise to unkindly discover
the scale of the feeling we leave behind;
the hedgehog, in fact, who has just uncovered
that 'one big thing' between lovers and us.

Wake

That dream again – you hadn't stayed
but crossed a life from side to side
and painted out its picture. I start,
and cast the darkness for sense.
But the clock-light is runic,
and the shadows will not realise,
and I would not wake you to check you here;
though I do not hear you breathe,
or feel your touch, you have not gone.
We have simply turned aside to sleep.

Here Are Some Words

Through the feint of the half-light,
you are leaving our bed, and stepping out
of the circle that marks what we know
from what we will measure apart.
Outside, the weather has woken,
and brushed the streets with yesterday's rain.
But the water on the window is too much,
and overcomes all vision; and if I do not blink
it is only to keep the wave from breaking.
Because I will not leave the circle; because
you are my fingertips, my perfect sight,
an acre of wheat in a field of stone.
Every time I close my eyes
this is what I'll see.

Election

When they ask you, you will say
that you only did as anyone would:
retreat to what you know – in your case,
home – that pocket of the Thames, flowered spring,
to set the old frames standing.
Now, as the sun flares around the curtains,
you part the fabric an inch towards the day
and look out on the fields that stitch your life
to the world beyond, each square of earth
a stepping stone from where you are
to where you want to be.
Perhaps it is the way the light falls on the soil today,
but you swear you've never seen so far –
the almshouse and the shouldered church,
the flooded football pitch, the common
yoked in buttercups and cattle –
and further still: a ribbon of Thames,
a railway stealing on and out to London.
This day was spinning long before you stirred,
in the wildlife, in the tilt of the earth;
it will turn despite the choice you have to face.
How small we are to make so much
of all that goes unnoticed by anyone but us.
Yet between the patterning of red wine and
cigarettes is the sense of damage –
of rarity cast-off the rounding world.
Such gifts were passed from hand to hand,
and then set down; such light lamped into darkness.
No longer sure which brings the bigger flicker –
the strike, or the extinction – but there is,
you think, in all of us an urge to set
the black blood free, a terrible need for breakage.

How the body keeps us bound you'll never know,
but you feel you've finally returned to yours
and made yourself your own.
And standing now at the reach of summer,
a tractor fastens one field to another,
and the land is voting for *change change*,
poppied with placards, electing time,
wanting your mark beside somebody's name.
You close your eyes, and figure the landscape
that is implacably your own:
the Gravel Pits and Beggarsbush,
the beds of watercress, the ride down Rabbits Hill.
So much will fall about you, but not this –
your place from harm, your echo room.
But half-way leaving town, you hit the brakes
and slow, and look in the mirror
for the rear view, for the world inversed,
its wrong turns and jumbled signs,
infinite stretch of opposites;
and you realise what's brought you to.
There is no choice less painful than the rest,
just a cleft between what's good, and what is best.
Which is what you will say, when they ask you.
As overhead, a pulse comes down the harness
from another town, towards your house,
towards your phone, where it hesitates
then echoes in an empty home.

Fake

– you say, and shed your fur across the chair.
As if you would, as if you'd touch 'the real beast' –
what is it these people take you for? And this,
a coat from your father, having days before
measured his length beside the church:
a broken toe, a key-hole bruise of a nose.

A dozen miles and two turns up the Thames
punts jigger as we giggle out
to the far boats and slip the knot
nudging each one off
like cattle we're sending home.

He's slowing down, you say, *my father.*
Though frankly I was enjoying the picture
of a single punt stealing downriver
for the Waterman's Reach, the Folly Bridge
and out for some black shire field

where a fake fox stops at a head-wind
chased by fake hounds.

Making a Killing

Our uncle had *made a killing* – he told us so.
A black and white Morris, a *Thirteen*-hundred,
gleaming as a just-sucked humbug.
Boys, he beamed, *they were giving it away.*

So there's us, my brother and me, for once
not fighting on the backseat, awed by the cigarette-
lighter, the electric de-mister, the state-of-the-art
AM radio crackling the way out to Grandpa's farm.

A fox had come trapped in the chicken run.
Smattered and feathered it ran mazy all morning,
half-mad with the fight of things.

Resting his gun, cocked against the back wall,
Grandpa rolled up his sleeves, stepped into the run,
and beat it to death with his hands.

We came away in silence, our uncle
tuned to the road ahead as if no longer with us.
My brother said that if you looked back
you saw gunlock,
                    spark –
                              and Grandpa,
framed in the backseat window, moving
through smoke with a draggle of things,
burning the least of the chickens.

One Man Went to Mow

I

This morning McGrandle was up before sunrise,
dressing in silence, with nothing so much as a glance
at his dog, or his wife. And taking his sickle
from the kitchen table, his scythe from the wall
where it hung by the lariat, he slipped the bolt
to the back and stepped out, and headed up to the meadow.

And this morning, like the last and the one before that,
he waded out where the grass stood tall as himself;
and flushing the dew between forefinger, thumb,
he nodded, as if to his dog. Finally, it has begun.

*

Not owning a boat, my father took work
on the land, and a cottage tied but empty
since Donnell had died leaving his wife
two boys too young to pick up his scythe.
The farmer came not with a cart, but his dogs,
and by daybreak the Donnells were gone.

My father, buffed with his luck, spoke only
of the farmer's fairness; who afterall had given him
no less than a roof and wages where a man was known
by his work, or he wasn't known at all.

II

There were two men on the field today.
Wilson, having yesterday noted McGrandle,
came over the marsh and past the yard where I
was splitting wood. And should he have brought his dog
he would have been reminded that he was but
the second man out to mow. And so

he tethered the cur to a gate and came alone.
And with nothing so much as a word between them
the men rode out in the meadow.
And by sundown the leeward was shorn.

*

Long after my father could work the field
he kept the sickle his father handed down
whetted, rolled up in a cloth by the sink.
Mornings had him lapping the blade, honed
to a point so keen the air would quiver
as he taught me the arc of his swing.

Not yet old enough to span the handle
I'd run the gat and burn of the riverbank, checking
the traps for knapped rabbits; my father closing
the cloth on his sickle, petal by wintering petal.

III

The boy had died when the orchard wall fell in.
Roberts came for his son, found him maculate,
a windfall he carried home and buried,
simply, out by the brook. And if he shook
with grief or anger we should not have known;
for no one went over the karren to see him.

And with nothing so much as an afternoon passing
he was back on the fields, as he was this morning;
which reminds of this and the following:
that after him comes Jameson, and after him comes me.

*

It began with a twinge in the threshing season
and by winter it was clear that my father's spine
was rotting. The farmer had come with a deal:
he would keep us in home and keep us in cider
if I would work off the debt. And with that my father,
not knowing a comeback, passed me ungently as cattle.

And surely at this, a moment of taking stock,
there should be some line about backbone. But suffice
it to say that here a young boy's mind was set forever:
that the only scythe that I would raise would be in anger.

IV

Last night I dreamt I took the road to Darlem;
and that out of the smirr came McGrandle,
his lantern raised and fizzing. And he told of a ship
whose prow within a prow was said to stow
a discreet cargo of travellers. And he spoke
of work throwing nets at sea, of families

with mothers and daughters. And the road
seemed to kite on the hill before me.
And Wilson and Roberts stopped to put down
their harrow and point at a rabbit in a tree.

And circling his house for a door, the farmer
stopped to point at the rabbit in the tree.
And Jameson sat down to write a poem
that began with a rabbit in a tree.
And only my father, having felt my going,
looked up from what he was doing, and hollered,

'Son, do you remember this one? –'
And he sang a tune I learned from young,
a counting song that we numbered into the dozens;
which up until then I had thought ascended for ever.

Our Father

Before we give this back, a last run –
in Tuscany's patchwork of conifer,
terracotta and vine. Our hire car will limp
from incline to incline; a snaketail
of Fiats passing, sunwild,
on the camber up to the hairpin.

We have come too late for the sunflowers:
field on field bowed in the heat
like so many heads in prayer. And you,
padding the wayside in your 'Hundred Yard Hat',
seeking more Heavenly intervention
than the rain, the fucking rain –

But then, let's not mess about here
with suggestion and marginalia.
And no allusions, no clever connections
to the wilting of flowers and a
whispering of, say, The Lord's Prayer:
from here, it's strictly secular.

And who really cares if a flower
makes it to winter but the profane,
most casual, observer?

The Wash

All summer the rainfall was biblical.
Seawater, nightly, brought gifts to our door:

crab claws and hawser, a boat on the highstreet,
roads leading into the sea.

Each day the reach had been rising
and those who had seen it before

were talking of *waterslain* –
a flooding so surely as nightfall

sweeping a coastline to sea.
We filled the car with what we could:

our two cats, that pair of clocks,
heads alive with flood-lore –

who put the kerf on Friary roof,
who lost his wife but not one single book.

And, for a moment, it's upon us –

We have taken the boat to the river,
toggled a path to the edge of the water
and put down where trout shoehorn at our feet.
In this boat bellied with paintpeel and moss
I will guide us upriver, away from the flood,
with a sackful of things clutched up
in the hours at dawn.

And husbands will call to their children
to come in off the field, come in
and wash for their tea. And they'll come
mud-faced and scrambling stories
of water, great water, climbing the hill.
And wives will flight from their fishing-boats
smelling of rockwind and kelp
and stand ashen, ashen; or plashing
through rooms with sandbags and peat sod
scooping up kids from the runnels.

There will be no maps for where we are,
but a swirl of haybale, splints of timber,
cattle bloating in the current.

And later, much later,
the water will come from all sides at once
and our boat will welter and coup.

And in that moment I will hold you under.
Your face will moon from the water.

*

I have seen it inside you,

                    a cue ball

where part of your head should be.
You carry the thing sewn up in your skull,

the sound of the sea trapped in
and trickling through shunts;

if you opened your mouth
seabirds would peck out your tongue.

You have sat with a friend who has it too
in cigarette clouds and silence;
                              and yet
nothing rhymes with cancer –
and this strange company is no company at all

but a waiting room of small arrangements –
the saltings turning with the aster, samphire;

the shoals of Thief Sand, Black Buoy Knock;
the boats spilling their nets off the Staithe,

a shale of oysters, lobster pots,
mussels torn out of the creek.

Tonight I scoop you from an empty bath,
naked as whale bone

                              left high on the tide,
and know by now what it is.

It's not the flood I fear but what comes after –
the endless roaming to find a home

like Shuck, the Viking dog, who beats
by legend a nightpath over these marshes

looking for a boat that's long pulled out,
to find place in the heart of nothing.

Passing Place

In the year before the year
before you died
we threaded our Ford

rainward –
foot by foot
up through the pass

of the Brecons,
tuning out of the radio
and all known language.

We were leaving England
on a car-width
cut out of the bluff

slewing back
for the pass
scooped into the hill

or rolling a wheel
on the hummock
and bog

at roadsigns
we could
no longer decipher.

But then language
was layering,
you would say,

going down
for the good words
which lay

just under the tongue –
not in phrasebooks
or schoolrooms

but the mor
and mull
of the language –

the loam of ourselves
tilled over,
grown in.

All day we went back
for the siding,
for the wide road

for the strange
communion
of each car by –

hand after hand
held up
to mine;

all day, back
for the roadsigns
ringing the cwm –

the PASSING PLACE
and what it was
in Welsh.

There are places
at which we stop,
pearl white

the rain in our mouth,
where we leave
language behind.

MAN PASIO.
As if we could
translate.

The Stoneman

A type, mind, is a little man;
a face, a beard, shoulders and arms,
look – even the shank of a body.

           – A.R. SPALDING, The Mannerisms of Type

I

A true navigator, he could course
the old print-works from memory –
decoding a world of picas and rubies,
of going to the case for brevier, bourgeois;
lining the back-to-front type, sort by sort,
or leading the galley for the optimum gauge;
before taking the chase to the stoneman
who'd dress it with furniture, sidesticks, quoins,
measuring the gutters and locking the forme for press.

A world of infinite detail, he learned
to tell founts by the slightest flourish:
the kern of an f, or the spur on a G –
those stubby descenders of Goudy,
those Baskerville *J*s, Fournier *z*s,
and the crazed swash of Caslon, Garamond.
He would scour the cases for dog's cocks, ampersands,
the Old Face of Blado–Poliphilus;
drumming-up scraps on the origins of *out of sorts*;
how we take *upper* and *lower* case
from the height at which the type was stored.

To handle the language like that –
to lift, assured, each letter into place,
knowing it either clean or dissed
(one or the other, no in-between);

and throwing the frocked type for the recast
when the paraffin no longer did the trick.

And yet, more than aware of composing a line
that would soon be lifted and distributed,
so that nothing he worked would survive him
only its residue: imposed, in print, out of it.

In the same way, his men are scattered now, far flung
or melted down, leaving only the legacy:
of how as a young devil some wag would send him
for skyhooks, striped ink, an italic space,
or the old long weight. And what after all
did the 0 say to the 8, but *I like your belt*.

II

'The, ah, thing, you know,
that goes with the mongoose,
no, mouse, no. Ah.'
                              Again.
'The thing, *this* – '
(triangular shape w. hands)
'and the thing, *this* – '
(rectangular shape w. hands)
'and I want some. Okay?'

Far from okay, it's November
and you've talked this way since March –
raffling for nouns, what my compositor
would call *a pie*, all out of sorts,
your galley of the swapped-around.

THANK   :   GOD
how it makes you smile to hear yourself say

that you've fed the briefcase or the mantelpiece;
and, in its way, how eloquent that
booting your laptop 'manufactures the sky'.

But you're tongued-tied, belted,
deported from language, to where
'there are almost no zooms', or 'orange nose bags';
going to the place of 'the three easy ones',
the 'head-grind tea', or some such else;

and five miles out of surgery, your head still newly sewn –
'When will the stonecutter come to cut the stone?'

III

Let me set this line the way you want it,
and lay the letters you would choose –
no damaged characters or battered type
no sort in need of planing,
no widows & orphans but the right fount:
sheer measure, aligned, and no omissions.

All we want is to draw a little proof from the world;
from time to time, catch sight of ourselves
in the printer's mirror and say we set it right,
before moving on to the stoneman
to leave his indelible mark;

so that long after the inking
and the distributing of sorts
what is left is binding, an impression, and paper.

One

I've come to realise this:
that the past, I think,

is not behind us
but somewhere else;

untellable, a curve away.
                        One day

we will surely pull into ourselves,
meeting-up   in loop

as negatives
laid onto each other.

Until then we will carry on
tracing each thing

that passes in the dark,
sifting the embers

for clues and warmth,
to keep among us what has gone;

like the garden we wake to
after a night-pour:

cobwebs of water
a saucer of rain.